The Art of Letter Writing

BY

A Society Lady

with a specially-written section on

LOVE, COURTSHIP, AND MARRIAGE

Bodleian Library
UNIVERSITY OF OXFORD

This edition first published in 2014 by the Bodleian Library,
Broad Street, Oxford, OX1 3BG
www.bodleianbookshop.co.uk

ISBN: 978 1 85124 397 6

Cover design by Dot Little
Designed and typeset by JCS Publishing Services Ltd in 10.75
on 13.75 pt Electra font
Printed and bound in China by C&C Offset Printing Co. Ltd
on 100gsm YuLong pure 1.3 paper
British Library Catalogue in Publishing Data
A CIP record of this publication is available from the British
Library

Contents

The Art of Letter Writing

Just before the War it was customary to regard letter writing as a lost art, certainly one in which few excelled as did the Early Victorians.

During the War, however, the art was revived in a most extraordinary manner among all classes, and some of the letters written from the battlefields are destined to endure as literature. But generally there is no gainsaying the fact that modern correspondence is characterized by a brusqueness and brevity which do not compare favourably with the leisurely grace, neatly-turned sentences and ceremonious style of our slower-going ancestors.

The necessity which impelled the latter to write ten to twenty pages no longer exists. The post, the railway, the telephone, the telegraph, wireless, and the motor-car, to say nothing of the aeroplane, enable friends and members of families constantly to keep in close touch with each other.

THE MISSION OF A LETTER WRITER.

There are many people who find themselves at a loss when called upon to deal by correspondence with some subject with which they are not fully conversant; besides, these are days when it is to the interest of everyone to economize time and trouble. A carefully classified selection of representative letters, which, by a few simple modifications, may be adapted to meet an infinite number of cases, will be found, therefore, invaluable to the busy correspondent.

It is not suggested that the letters set forth here should be transcribed literally; they are draft letters, intended to serve as guides and as models.

Address and Date.

The address should be full and distinct; the date should likewise be added clearly.

The headings of business letters are usually printed, the address is given in full, and the postal district of the metropolis is added.

Business communications which are typed should be signed in ink by the writers. Unless to very intimate friends and on rare occasions, typewritten private letters should not be forwarded without some sort of apology.

The Commencement.

The greeting or "salutation" may vary considerably. In communications between mere acquaintances the style varies from "Sir" to the familiar "My dear —". "My dear" is generally regarded, and particularly when the communication is between a lady and gentleman, as savouring of a certain intimacy. The more usual form is "Dear Mr. — and Dear Miss —, or Mrs. —," as the case may be.

The Impersonal Style.

The following manner of address may be adopted: "Mrs. Jones presents her compliments to Mrs. Smith and will feel obliged if she will be so good as to return the books," etc.

Care must be taken in these cases that the relative positions of the writer and recipient are not altered, for the pronouns are apt to get mixed in inexperienced hands, and it is difficult to know which lady is indicated by "her" and by "she." The third person must be used all through.

Business Letters.

The commencements of business letters admit of slight variation. The formal is here the most polite and, indeed, the most convenient style, as business letters necessarily pass through many hands. For this reason, if for no other, nothing but the subject actually in hand should be mentioned in business correspondence. If social letters are to be written to business men, it is more polite to send them to the private residence of the person for whom they are intended; or, at least, in a note separate from the business letter, marked "Private".

In addressing gentlemen of any position, it is usual and courteous to write them *Esq.* (not Esquire in full), and never "*Mr.*" So-and-So. It is better to err on the side of over-politeness than to run a risk of offending.

Write distinctly, and do not write across your letters.

PUNCTUATION.

Punctuation is an important, but generally disregarded, feature of correspondence. The relative value of the "stops" should be learned, and the proper use of the hyphen, the inverted commas, and the parenthesis ought to be studied.

COMPOSITION.

The formation of the sentences requires special attention. No doubt a sentence spoken ungrammatically is as bad as one written ungrammatically, but the latter remains as evidence of an error, and is consequently more regrettable.

Be natural, and do not strive after effect in your correspondence.

The correspondence which most nearly approaches conversation is invariably interesting, and if one writes as one speaks, all stiff, stilted phrases and meaningless comments or questions in a letter received will be abolished, and in their stead will be chatty details and personal news. The golden rule of letter writing is to adapt the manner and the matter to one's correspondent, and, observing this precept, one's letters breathe one's personality and are usually acceptable to their recipients.

The frequent underlining of words, and words of many syllables should be avoided.

The Conclusion.

The endings of social letters vary as much as the commencement, and business communications pure and simple, are also capable of variation. To intimate friends, ladies frequently sign them, "Yours affectionately"; but the more usual, and less pushing, and frequently the most sincere form is "Yours truly," or "Yours sincerely." "Yours very truly" is also common.

The following examples for the termination of various letters will explain themselves:—

1. The formal – Believe me, my dear Sir (or Madam), Yours faithfully (or respectfully);
2. The social – Believe me, my dear Sir (or Madam), Yours truly (or sincerely);
3. More intimate – I remain, dear Mrs. —, Yours sincerely (or truly);
4. Friendly – Believe me, my dear Frank, Ever truly yours (or sincerely your friend);
5. Affectionate – I am, my dearest Aileen, (Very) Affectionately yours.

There is a tendency, however, to omit the more formal "Believe me, my dear Sir," or "I remain, dear Mrs. —" and to sign oneself simply, "Yours faithfully," "Yours truly," or "Yours sincerely."

The signature of every letter should be particularly legible, as much time may be lost by a correspondent endeavouring to ascertain who and what the writer is. If a lady is married, it is as well sometimes to indicate the fact to a stranger by enclosing her card; or, as the Americans do, by putting Mrs. or Miss in brackets before her signature.

It is a breach of good taste to make use of any title or handle to one's name, although the use of such is sanctioned on the Continent and indulged in by some people in this country. A peer usually signs his title only.

CARE AND CONSIDERATION.

Hurried writing in social communications is to be deprecated. A clean, cool, well-written letter, free from erasures and unsightly blots, implies consideration. (1) Weigh your words, and (2) Never exaggerate.

Rude or impertinent letters should never be written; if received, they should be ignored.

Never pretend, in correspondence, to be a solicitor. To do so is an actionable offence.

To seek to give specimen letters designed to meet *all* the requirements of the delicate and varied class of correspondence which might be grouped under the various Sections of the Letter Writer would be not only to attempt the impossible, but to set out to fill volumes.

All we have had in mind has been in every Instance to present, as it were, a model, the form of which could be varied in manifold ways, to harmonize with the conditions of each particular case.

We trust we have succeeded in our aim; and that many who are capable of intense feeling, but have not the gift of expression, may find in the letters a hint, an idea, or a phrase which will set a train of thought in motion to the end desired.

SECTION I.

Love, Courtship, and Marriage
(By A. B.)

LETTER NO. 1.

From a Gentleman to a Lady, on Love at First Sight.

DEAR MISS B ——,

I am writing that which I fear I have not the courage, on so short an acquaintance, to tell you.

The moment you came into my life I loved you.

Before we met I did not believe love at first sight possible. But *you* opened my eyes, and caused me to see this wondrous truth in life—the sudden revelation of all that is lovely and divine in a human soul.

May I call on you? or will you consent to meet me?

Be as merciful as you are beautiful, and save from despair

Yours ever,

A. L. MARGRAVE.

Letter No. 2.

From a Lady to a Gentleman, asking him to refrain from Further Attentions.

DEAR MR. DASHAWAY,

I now feel it necessary to write you on a matter which has caused me some concern lately.

I refer to your persistent and, to me, very distasteful attentions.

I do not know that I have ever consciously given you any encouragement; and I am therefore hoping that, on receipt of this expression of my sentiments towards you, your gentlemanly instincts will prompt you to desist from what I cannot but consider an embarrassing annoyance.

Yours truly,
BERYL ROSS.

Letter No. 3.

From an Absent Gentleman to his Fiancée.

MY DEAREST KATHLEEN,

I am eagerly grasping the first moment's leisure of the day to again say how much I love you.

The thought of you is so constantly with me that I find it difficult at any time to wholly fix my attention to the task I have in hand.

All things beautiful suggest *you*. As I write, I catch the sound of distant music—and at once the charm of your low, sweet voice steals over me. A fair face passes my window—and instantly I recall all your loveliness and grace.

Yesterday a tiny flower fell at my feet. Because it was of the kind *you* love, I saved its delicate life; and now, as its fragrance compels my notice, it seems, in its purity and freshness, a perfect symbol of you.

How dull and empty the evening hours are without you! And how frequently at these times do I conjure up a vision of the home that is to be, with *you* by my side— cheerful, helpful, and inspiring, and never wearying in your effort to make it a veritable heaven on earth.

Send me an assurance of your love by return. Tell me all that is in your heart as you read this and always think of me as

Your devoted
STEPHEN.

Letter No. 4.

From a Lady Very Much in Love to her Absent Fiancé.

My dearest Ronald,

No sooner had we parted than I began to count the hours that must drag through their weary course ere you could return to me.

For long past we have each understood there has been no need for anything in the nature of reserve between us; and so I feel I may reveal to you, dear, my inmost thoughts as I write.

I sometimes wonder do many girls love as I and are other men to them also merely shadows, passing to and fro in their lives.

It is a wonderful and a beautiful thing this love of mine for you. It seems to quicken all my thoughts and feelings.

When *you* are near, the world is at once transformed into a place where there is no room for sorrow, pain, or fear—only for hope and peace and a great, glad sense of truly living.

Come back to me quickly, dearest; for I need you as the flowers the sunshine and the dew.

Restore my joyous world to me. Without you it is a sad and dreary place for

Yours through time and eternity,
Violet.

Letter No. 5.

From a Gentleman Pleading for Forgiveness after a Lovers' Quarrel.

My dearest Love,

I cannot rest until I have written imploring forgiveness for leaving you so abruptly, and in such jealous anger.

What your thoughts to-day must be of me I dare not imagine. I have nothing to say by way of excuse for my churlish behaviour. Only do I ask for pardon.

You may not know, dear, but at times your beauty, your grace, your intelligence, and the witching charm of your voice, all seem to unite in a conspiracy to rob me of reason.

That you will send me a reply at once, and restore me to the paradise of your trusting love, is the feverish wish of

Yours very sorrowfully,
Fred.

Lady's Reply to Lover's Letter Asking for Forgiveness after a Quarrel.

My dear Sidney,

Your penitent letter reached me at a moment when life seemed very dull and uninteresting; but, thank Heaven, all is bright and hopeful again.

Forgive you! Why, you dear old boy, I never thought you needed pardon.

I knew full well the reason of your anger, which, after all, was in itself indirect evidence of the great love you have for me. Though I sometimes wish you would *try* to understand my sex better—and myself in particular.

You should remember that a woman can give her whole heart to one man (as I have to you), and yet be *very* agreeable to other men. You see, it is a woman's way.

Now, come to me as soon as possible; but do not mention a word of this distressing past. Just be your old, loving, attentive self again to

Yours only,

Edith.

Letter No. 7.

Proposal of Marriage.

DEAREST WINNIE,

The time has at last arrived when I feel I can ask you to be my wife.

I dared not do this until I had assured our future. But now I am able to offer you a home—perhaps not worthy of you (a palace would not, in my estimation, be that), yet a home full of modest comfort, and one which your very presence would, I know, make beautiful.

You cannot guess what the hope of one day being able to call you *wife* has been to me. When at times I have grown weary in the battle of life, it has given me new strength and courage, and has enabled me to accomplish much I thought well-nigh impossible.

This being so, what might I not achieve under the inspiration of your *constant*, loving companionship?

Send me the answer I so earnestly desire. Then in all this wide world there will be no happier man than

Yours, for ever,

ROBERT.

Letter No. 8.

Reply to Proposal of Marriage.

My dearest Jack,

I find it difficult to express all the varied emotions your letter has excited in me to-day.

Will I consent to become your wife? Let me confess, this would be the crowning joy of my life.

When I reflect on the happy time we have already passed together; when I recall your many acts of unselfish kindness to me; and, above all, the chivalrous respect you have for all women, I feel I need have no fear in trusting my future happiness to your keeping.

I know that the close intimacy of the marriage state calls for the exercise of qualities demanded by no other condition in life—especially those of patience and forbearance.

But you can trust me, Jack. It will be my constant endeavour to make myself more than a wife to you. I will seek to be also a helpful, cheerful companion—proud of you, proud of my home, and ever striving to make it for *you* a "haven of rest".

Come to me, as soon as possible, for there is so much I would say to you that I feel I cannot write.

Ever your loving
Irene.

From Gentleman, Breaking off Engagement.

DEAR DORA,

It is with something more than reluctance that I am about to perform what I feel to be a duty to you and to myself.

I have to tell you that I realize *I no longer love you.* Indeed, I am not certain that I ever did — in the way you so well deserve to be loved.

What can I say in explanation? Only this: You have a manner so captivating that, quite unconsciously, you draw others to yourself (and especially the opposite sex) almost against their will. Any man thrown constantly in your society (as I have been) might, after a time, imagine he loved you.

But circumstances have lately revealed to me the true feeling I have for you—and I am very sure it is not love.

I do not think I should have had the courage to tell you this, were it not that I have never been wholeheartedly certain of your affection for myself.

You see, it is second nature with you to be gracious and kind to all men, and this fact may have deceived *me.*

I pray it is so, and that in releasing me from the engagement there will be nothing of sorrow on your part; only, as with myself, a passing regret.

While wishing you abundant happiness in the future, may I ask you to always think of me as

Your sincere friend,

ALFRED?

LETTER NO. 10.

From a Lady, Breaking off Engagement.

DEAR JIM,

I am writing to ask you to do a thing which I fear will give you pain, but which, after very close communion with myself, I have decided will be best for us both. *I wish you to free me from my engagement.*

I will be perfectly frank with you. I now know that I never really loved you, and that it was the ardour of your love for *me* more than any true affection on my part which compelled my consent to become your wife.

Here let me say that if ever a woman respected a man, I do you, for I know your sterling qualities.

But respect is not love, and marriage without love would to me seem a mockery.

I think you understand me well enough to believe that I am not the kind of girl to lightly make such a decision, especially realizing, as I do, how much it means to you.

So forgive me if I have hurt you, and do allow me to consider myself always

Your sincere friend,

AMINA.

LETTER No. 11.

From Gentleman to Friend, Announcing Marriage.

DEAR WALTER,

At last the happiest man in the world is writing to tell you he has married the sweetest woman on earth.

I can see your genial smile at this. But *you* do not yet know by personal experience what is meant by "the joys of matrimony".

Think of it, old boy! After a hard, fagging day's work, to return to a home neat, bright, and with every sign of simple comfort! And, above all, presided over by a cheerful, dainty, ministering angel.

If you are in any way sceptical, come and see us, old friend, at the very earliest opportunity. Be prepared to stay a day or so; and I am convinced you will leave a convert, and with a firm resolve to do likewise.

With very pleasant recollections of the many "good times" we have had together in my bachelor days, and kindest regards from Isabel,

I remain, as of old,
Fraternally yours,
ALBERT.

LETTER NO. 12.

From Gentleman Friend, Offering Congratulations.

DEAR ALBERT,

Your very welcome note, announcing your marriage, came safely to hand this morning. Hearty congratulations, old chap!

Not yet having a very intimate acquaintance with the lady, I will take all you have said of her for granted.

Your kind invitation I will gladly accept, and you may expect me over at the present weekend.

I believe, old chum, I am your senior by a few years, and this, perhaps, will supply me with an excuse for writing to you—well, seriously.

As I am neither in love nor recently married, I naturally look at life through a more matter-of-fact pair of spectacles than your own. Not that I would wish it otherwise with you—at present.

But the time will come when familiarity with the joys of which you now so glowingly write will have a tendency to lessen your appreciation of them.

Then, Albert, it will be well for you if you try to remember the glamour of to-day. If you say, "I will, so far as in me lies, *remain* the attentive, considerate, lover-husband." So will the inevitable trials, vexations, and sorrows of married life lose half their sting, and so will you have reason to bless the day that made it possible for you to send me the letter which has prompted this reply.

Now, old fellow, don't exclaim, "Whatever can have happened to him?" It was only a momentary digression, as you will find when you again grip the hand of

Your sincere friend,
WALTER.

SECTION II.

Invitations for Visits to Country House or Seaside, Etc.

Invitation for a Country-House Visit, to Meet People of Some Position.

THE TOWERS,
INGELSBURGH,
DERBYSHIRE.
(Date in full.)

MY DEAR CÆCILIA,

May I hope that you will give us the pleasure of seeing you next month? We are having a little house-party for a week, from the 15th of October, and shall be delighted if you will come and make one of our party. We are expecting Mr. and Mrs. J——, Sir W. and Lady B——, the Hon. Emily W——, Jack Helyard Captain Somers, and the two Walkinghame boys We hope to have a picnic or two if the weather will be kind, or some sort of excursions, and of course they will be getting up something in the way of charades or acting of some kind. I believe you have met Jack before, and the Walkinghames are very nice boys. Do manage to come. We shall be sending brakes down to the station any time between 2 and 5 p.m., or of course, any time later that you name. We dine on the 15th at 8 o'clock.

> Looking forward to seeing you,
> Yours affectionately,
> JANE FERRARS.

Invitation for a Quiet, Friendly, Country Visit.

OAK LODGE,
SELLINGHAM,
NEAR CHESTER.
(Date in full.)

MY DEAR MARY,

John asked me the other day if you were not soon coming to see us again—it seems such a long time since we saw you—so I want to say to him that you are coming very soon! When may I say? Can you come before the end of the month and give us a few weeks? We shall both be so very pleased if you can. The country is looking so lovely now; the banks along the Framley Road are covered with foxgloves nearly to the top of the hedges—they are a sight for sore eyes indeed—and the hay will soon be cut; and I want you to come and see our roses before they begin to go off. Does not all that tempt you? John is frightfully pleased with a new pony he has lately bought, and I know he wants to drive you from the station so that you can admire it properly. I had to give you that little hint beforehand! Well, dear! just write and say which day will suit you—how about the 25th? But name any day so that it is not too far off and with every good and warm regard from us both,

Yours very affectionately,
NELLIE SOMERS.

Reply to Invitation to a Quiet Country Visit.

42, HASLEMERE ROAD,
SHEFFIELD.
(Date in full.)

MY DEAREST NELLIE,

Your dear kind letter is tempting me most fearfully. I don't know whether I ought to leave just now, for the Vicar's wife is not very well, and she is relying upon me for her girls' sewing class and the mothers' meeting. However, as the 25th gives me ten days, I shall be off from parish work from then, and come and feast my eyes on the foxgloves and your roses—I can smell the hay already! The attraction of seeing you and John is, of course, quite secondary to the roses and the foxgloves! I hope you have heaps of news for me. I shall want to be posted up in all the gossip of the neighbourhood. How is Mrs. Jones's rheumatism? and do Mrs. Jennings's hens lay properly? and have you yet found a suitable helpmeet for the new curate? You see that the very thought of coming to you is making me frivolous already! You have much on your conscience! Au revoir! With love to you both (*may* I send my love to John?),

> Yours ever as ever,
> MARY BROADINGS

Inviting a Friend to a Visit in Writer's own House.

> LESLIE HOUSE,
> AUGUSTA GARDENS,
> TORQUAY.
> (*Date in full.*)

MY DEAR JENNIE,

It seems such long ages since I have seen anything of you, and I am sure a fortnight down here would be very good for you, and I am still more sure that it would be very good for me, and for all of us. So I want to know if you cannot arrange to come and pay us a little visit next month. You know, without my telling you, how delighted we shall all be to have you among us again. We were all so very sorry to hear of Jack's accident; I do hope he has quite got over it, and no evil result left behind. Please give him our very sincere and warm remembrances. I expect you will find Milly and John grown nearly out of knowledge; they wish me to send their love, and are looking forward to seeing you next month. And with my own keen anticipation of your visit and much love,

Believe me, dear,

Yours always affectionately,

EMILY J. BLACKSTAFF

Inviting a Friend to Join the Writer in Hotel or House Rented for the Season.

—— HOTEL,

BOURNEMOUTH.

(Date in full.)

MY DEAREST BARBARA,

We came down here two weeks ago, and can hardly tell you how much better we are feeling already. The place is as delightful as ever, and we want you to come and join us. Give us a fortnight of yourself. Do come, and as soon as you can possibly get away. I am sure it will do you good, and I feel sure I may say I think you will enjoy being here. We have been lucky in getting very comfortable quarters, and mean to make a fairly long stay; but we want you. We met Cicely M —— a few days ago and her fiancé: they seem to have a party down here; also Sir James H ——, all alone; and I hear the Browne-Brownes are coming next week. Now, do write and say "Yes"; and if you will say what day, and by what train you will come, we will send to meet you at the station, and shall look forward to a jolly time. Au revoir!

Yours always, with love,
(*or* affectionately, *or* very sincerely),
MARGARET

Answer to Invitation to Seaside from a Friend.

TIMBUCTOO HOUSE,
LANCASTER ROAD,
ST. ALBANS,
HERTS.
(Date in full.)

MY DEAREST MARGARET,

How very kind of you! Thank you so much for your kind invitation. I shall be so very pleased to come and be with you and yours again, and enjoy a whiff of sea air—it is getting frightfully prosy here—and I have been thinking of you all lately, and longing for a good old cosy chat. It is lovely to be able to look forward to a pleasant time with you again. I have only been to Bournemouth once before, and I liked the place very much then. My mother has not been very well lately, and Katie has been away, staying with her friends at Lowestoft, but we expect her back the beginning of next week; and if it would suit you for me to come about the end of the week—say, Friday, by the train leaving Victoria at 2.20 p.m.—I shall be looking forward to it with the greatest pleasure. If any other day or hour would suit you better, please do not hesitate to let me know. Till we meet, and with lots of love,

Yours ever affectionately,
BARBARA L ——.

Invitation for a Christmas Visit (Town or Country).

(ADDRESS IN FULL.
Date in full.)

MY DEAREST SALLIE,

We all want you to come and help us to spend Christmas this year. Will you come on the 23rd and give us a week? The boys come home that day, and if you can conveniently join their train, or, say, arrive about the same time, James can meet you all and bring your luggage together; but if that does not quite fit in with your plans, never mind: we can soon fix up whatever will meet you. So you see I am not contemplating any refusal! We are having the cousins Tom and Harry, and also a nice school friend of Janet's, so shall be, I hope, a merry party. We are intending a children's party, and a grown-up dance, and some acting, and we are all looking forward to having you amongst us—so don't *think* of anything otherwise. With love from us all,

Your always affectionate friend,
KITTY PERSHORE.

Invitation for a Visit to Town in the Season.

GROSVENOR HOUSE,
EATON GARDENS, W. 19.
(Date in full.)

MY DEAR CHARLOTTE,

It will give me so very much pleasure if your dear mother can spare you to come and spend two or three weeks with us in May. Julia is looking forward to the Season, and there will be several very good concerts, as well as some large parties, and I believe some houseboat parties, and it will be a great pleasure to Julia as well as to me if you will come and let me take you about with us. If you will come, I shall have a maid for you and Julia, as my own maid Céleste will scarcely be able to manage for the three of us; and I want you to have a really nice time. Please give my love to your dear mother, and with Julia's love and my own to your very dear self,

Believe me,
Your affectionate friend,
ISOBEL MYERS.

Invitation to Join a Motor Tour.

THE MANOR HOUSE,
WALLABY,
WORCESTERSHIRE.
(Date in full.)

DEAREST GERALDINE,

Will you come and join us in a motor tour? George is frightfully proud of a new car he has just got—it is rather a ducky one and *very* comfy—and we want to have a really nice jolly tour about Wales. If you can come—and we are tremendously set on your joining us—there will be you, and George and myself, and my brother Frank. I think you *have* met Frank—anyway, he is quite sure he remembers you—so we ought to make a nice little party. We thought of starting from here about the first of next month. George thinks of mapping out the tour beforehand; but of course it can be changed if anybody has any suggestions to make—but he will find out beforehand where are the best hotels and stopping-places. Will you say which day you can come? Let it be a few days before we start, won't you? so that we can settle things and get off comfortably. With love,

Yours in anticipation of a jolly time,
FREDA.

Reply to Invitation to Motor Tour.

THE CEDARS,
LETCHFORD,
BUCKS.
(Date in full.)

DARLING FREDA,

How jolly! and how good of you to ask me to join you! I shall love it of all things! and do tell George to manage to get the Clerk of the Weather in a good temper! Tell me what wraps I shall want, and about how long do you propose to be "on tour"? I hope you mean to include Carnarvon and Bettws-y in your programme; there are such heaps of lovely places in Wales, one wants to include them all. I suppose you will go to Tintern and Chepstow and Raglan—but I am being a selfish pig, and *you* must choose your route. Wherever you take me, I shall be quite happy. Suppose I come to you on the 28th, will that quite suit you? and will you tell me by what train to arrive at Wallaby?

Yours, quite jumpy with joy,
GERALDINE BLACKLEY

SECTION III.

Invitations to Dinners, Concerts, and Dances, Etc.

Formal Invitation to Dinner.

Mr. and Mrs. William Henderson request the pleasure of Mr. and Mrs. Jamieson's company at dinner on Thursday, the 22nd inst., at half-past seven o'clock.

THE HOLLOW,
April 12th.

Mr. and Mrs. Jamieson have much pleasure in accepting Mr. and Mrs. William Henderson's kind invitation to dinner for Thursday, the 22nd inst.

BEECH HOLME,
April 13th.

Mr. and Mrs. Jamieson much regret that owing to a prior engagement they are unable to accept Mr. and Mrs. William Henderson's kind invitation for the 22nd inst.

BEECH HOLME,
April 13th.

Invitation to a Dance.

DEAR MRS. JAMIESON,

Will you and Mr. Jamieson and your son and daughter give us the pleasure of your company at a dance we are giving on Thursday, the 20th inst.? Dancing will begin at nine o'clock.

Yours very sincerely,

MARY HENDERSON.

THE HOLLOW,
April 2nd.

DEAR MRS. HENDERSON,

Thank you so much for your kind invitation for Thursday, the 20th. I accept with much pleasure for Jennie and Arthur and myself. Mr. Jamieson begs to be excused, as his dancing days are over.

With kind regards,
Very sincerely yours,

ANNABEL JAMIESON.

BEECH HOLME,
April 3rd.

Less Formal Invitation to a Concert or
Dramatic Entertainment.

DEAR MRS. JAMIESON,

We are giving a little concert on Tuesday, the 15th inst., at 8.30 o'clock, and shall be so very pleased if you and Mr. Jamieson will favour us with your presence. We expect it to last about two hours.

Yours very sincerely,
MARY HENDERSON.

THE HOLLOW,
April 7th.

DEAR MRS. JAMIESON,

We are proposing to get up a little dramatic entertainment for Tuesday, the 15th inst., to begin at half-past eight o'clock. Will you and Mr. Jamieson and your daughter dine with us at seven o'clock, and give us the pleasure of your company for the evening?

Yours sincerely,
MARY HENDERSON.

THE HOLLOW,
April 7th.

Less Formal Invitation to Dramatic Entertainment.

DEAR MRS. JAMIESON,

My children are getting up a little dramatic entertainment for Tuesday, the 15th inst., to begin at half-past seven o'clock, and we shall be so glad if you and your young people will give us the pleasure of your presence for the evening.

Yours very sincerely,
MARY HENDERSON.

THE HOLLOW,
April 7th.

Reply.

DEAR MRS. HENDERSON,

My daughter and I will be delighted to come on Tuesday, the 15th, to dine and spend the evening. Mr. Jamieson regrets exceedingly that he must deny himself the pleasure of accepting your kind invitation, as he has an important meeting for that evening.

Yours very sincerely,
ANNABEL JAMIESON.

BEECH HOLME,
April 8th.

SECTION IV.

Business Letters.

*From Tenant to Landlord Respecting
Necessary Repairs.*

14, DENISON STREET,
INGLEFIELD.
(Date in full.)

DEAR SIR,

I shall be exceedingly obliged if you will kindly, and at your earliest convenience, take steps to have the water-spout mended on the west side of this house. There is a constant leakage, especially after heavy rain, with the result that the wall on that side is becoming permanently damp, and the damp is now penetrating through to the bedroom there. Also, I think a slate must be broken or loose near the chimney-stack, as the wet is coming through to the ceiling of the top front bedroom. May I hope you will kindly have these repairs attended to immediately, before we have any more heavy rains?

Yours truly

MARJORIE WINTERHOLME.

To MR. W. E. THORPE,
LONSDALE HOUSE.

To Landlord, Asking to be Released from Tenancy before Expiration of Lease.

MAYFIELD HOUSE,
WARMINSTER ROAD,
DONINGTON.
(Date in full.)

DEAR SIR,

As my husband has just accepted the management of some large works near to Bristol, we are anxious to move down into that neighbourhood as soon as possible, but our lease of this house has still, I know, three years to run. Will you be so very kind as to consider this, and let us know at your earliest convenience at what date, and on what terms, you would be prepared to release us from the remainder of our tenancy? We want, if possible, to get away by Lady Day, and will, of course, be ready to meet any reasonable terms you are kind enough to offer us. Regretting very sincerely that we find it necessary to make this move, and with our kind regards,

I am,
Yours sincerely,
MIRIAM BLOMFIELD

To JAMES WALLINGTON, ESQ.,
WALTON-CUM-BITCHLEY.

To Sanitary Inspector re Defective Drains, or re
Examination of Drains on Taking a House.

WILMINSTER HALL,
BICKERSTAFF.
(Date in full.)

DEAR SIR,

I shall be exceedingly obliged if you can make it convenient to call as soon as possible to inspect the drains here. I feel sure there must be a serious leakage or other grave defect connected with the scullery sink—there is unpleasantness there—and also we have had a good deal of illness in the house lately. I should be glad to have all the drains thoroughly inspected and certified in good order before signing lease for this house, which we are proposing to take on for some years longer. Will you kindly let me know how soon you can come?

I am,
Yours truly,
MARY JOLIFFE.

To MR. THOS. DICKSON,
INSPECTOR,
3, WORCESTER STREET.

To Lawyer, Asking Advice Respecting Payment for Necessary Sanitary Alterations.

WILMINSTER HALL,
BICKERSTAFF.
(Date in full.)

DEAR MR. CRAKE,

I am having a little trouble just now with my landlord about some very necessary sanitary alterations. We had several cases of illness at the Hall, and I called in the Sanitary Inspector, who has ordered some drastic alterations, which are, indeed, absolutely necessary. But as I was responsible for the Inspector's visit, the landlord wishes to charge us with half the cost of what has to be done. Will you kindly tell me what, under the circumstances, is our legal position with regard to cost of improved sanitation? Our three years' lease of the Hall is about expiring, and we are thinking of renewing it for seven years if the sanitation can be certified.

I am,
Yours sincerely,
MARY JOLIFFE.

WILLIAM CRAKE, ESQ.,
MESSRS. CRAKE, MARSTON
AND CRAKE,
LINCOLN'S INN SQUARE.

From Owner of House or Houses to House Agents.

SHENSTONE VILLA,
CANTERBURY ROAD,
NORTH KENSINGTON.
(Date in full.)

DEAR MR. WILLIAMS,

I hereby acknowledge receipt of rents for my houses Nos. 2, 4, 6, 8, in the Warwick Road for the quarter ending on June 24th, and am glad to note that these tenants are regular in their payments. I see that repairs are again required to the sink waste-pipe of No. 2, and to the kitchen ceiling and the roof of No. 4. On referring to my accounts with you, I find that the scullery sink at No. 2 was repaired only two months ago. Can you pull the tenants up about that, and suggest that there must surely have been careless usage on their part, or do you think the plumber was to blame? Will you kindly let me know what conclusion you come to? The work, however, must, of course, be done there, and to No. 4.

I am,
Yours truly,
JANE LESSING

To MR. WILLIAMS,
MESSRS. JEFFSON, WILLIAMS AND KNOX,
LEADBETTER LANE,
BATTERSEA.

To Landlord, Asking Time for Deferred Payment of Rent.

3, RAWSTONE VILLAS,
BLESSINGTON ROAD,
DITCHFIELD.
(Date in full.)

DEAR MR. WORTHINGTON,

I am exceedingly sorry to find that I must ask if you can and will possibly allow me to defer payment of rent due at Lady Day until the next quarter day, or I will, if possible, pay one-half of what is due at Lady Day in the middle of the ensuing quarter, and all that will then be due on Midsummer Day. With my husband's long illness, and unexpectedly heavy school bills for the children at Christmas, I am really quite unable to make up the rent this quarter. I very much regret having to make this request, and shall be grateful to you if you will accept this arrangement.

I am,
Yours very truly,
MLLLICENT BLANDFORD.

JAMES WORTHINGTON, ESQ.,
THE LODGE,
DITCHFIELD.

To Railway or Carrier Company Demanding Compensation for Goods Damaged in Transit.

THE HOMESTEAD,
LINDEN ROAD,
WATCHINGFORD.
(Date in full.)

SIR,

I sent a leather-covered trunk by your Company's carrier on Tuesday last, the 18th inst., from Richmond to this address. When delivered to the carrier it was perfectly sound and in good condition. Both my housemaid and the gardener who carried it downstairs can testify to this, and I think you will find your carrier will agree with them. When it was delivered here two days later, one handle was almost wrenched off and the lid nearly broken through—indeed, it is quite useless as it is. I shall be obliged if you will kindly say what you propose with regard to it, as the damage was done unquestionably while it was in your care.

I am.

Yours truly,

EMILY WHITEHEAD.

To the MANAGER,
MESSRS. THE L. AND S.W.
RY. COMPY.,
WATERLOO STATION.

To a Strange Doctor During Visit at the Seaside
or in the Country.

Mrs. Ritchies would be extremely obliged if Dr. Jeffson could make it convenient to call at Alma Villa some time to-day—as early as possible.

Mrs. Ritchies is a visitor in Bournemouth, and came down ten days ago with her daughter, and for the last two days Miss Ritchies has complained of headache and seems far from well. Mrs. Ritchies would be glad to have Dr. Jeffson's opinion as soon as possible.

When in town, Mrs. Ritchies' medical adviser is Dr. Blank Wemyss, of Harley Street.

ALMA VILLA,
ORPINGTON ROAD,
Tuesday morning.

SECTION V.

Applications for Appointments and Replies.

Application for Engagement as Responsible Housekeeper for a Gentleman.

Mrs. Wilson, having seen advertisement in *The Times* for a responsible housekeeper, writes to apply for the post. Mrs. Wilson has been a widow for the last ten years, and is fifty-four years of age. For the last five years she has been managing housekeeper with entire charge at Launds Hall, the residence of Lady Brown-Sengsford, with seven maid-servants, and where except for carrying coals, the work was all done by women-servants. Lady Brown-Sengsford is probably going abroad for some years, and Mrs. Wilson is looking out for a responsible position where the work will not be quite so heavy. Mrs Wilson has a thorough knowledge of cooking and the care of a gentleman's house, and feels sure she could make the advertiser very comfortable. She can refer to Lady Brown-Sengsford, and also encloses testimonials from gentlemen who have known her for many years. Salary £60.

LAUNDS HALL, JUMPINGTON.
(Date in full.)

Testimonial to Mrs. Wilson's General Character and Efficiency as Housekeeper.

I have pleasure in stating that, having known Mrs. Wilson and her varied circumstances intimately for the last thirty years, I have a very high opinion of her general character and capabilities. I believe her to be thoroughly high-principled and trustworthy. She brought up a family of four children, who are all a credit to their home, and she was a devoted and faithful wife. After losing her husband, her children being then all grown up, she took special lessons in cookery and attended some domestic science lectures, and for the last five years has acted as housekeeper for Lady Brown-Sengsford, who, I believe, found her most satisfactory. I knew her husband well, and her family; they were parishioners of mine for twenty years before her husband died, and I had the opportunity of seeing a great deal of Mrs. Wilson and of her husband and family, and I know that I am not alone in the parish in my very high opinion of her.

SELLINGTON RECTORY,
JUMPINGTONSHIRE.
(Date in full.)

Application for Post as Lady-Companion.

Miss Jones is writing in answer to advertisement from "A. B." in the *Church Times* of to-day for a lady-companion for an elderly lady who is becoming partially blind. Miss Jones is a lady and well educated, and a good reader, and has had considerable experience lately in the care of a house, and house-management generally, having been for five years companion-housekeeper for an invalid lady, who has now gone to live with her married daughter, and no longer requires a companion. Miss Jones is very practical and fond of gardening, and is forty-five years of age, and has very good health. She would be glad to learn further particulars of the engagement, and what salary is offered, and where the advertiser resides. If the advertiser considers this application, Miss Jones would be glad to meet her for personal interview at any hour and any place that is appointed.

15, LUDBOROUGH PLACE,
WEST MARLFORD.
(Date in full.)

*Enquiry Respecting Miss Jones, Applicant for
Post as Lady-Companion.*

Mrs. Dane-Watford presents her compliments to Mrs. Fellingborough, and writes to make enquiries respecting Miss Jones, who is applying for an engagement as lady-companion to Mrs. Dane-Watford's mother, Mrs. Westerton, who is partially blind and unable to write herself. Miss Jones states that she lived with Mrs. Felling-borough for five years as companion-housekeeper, and had much of the management of the house in her hands then. Will Mrs. Felling-borough kindly say if she considers Miss Jones trustworthy, a pleasant companion, and a lady in the usual sense of the word? As Mrs. Westerton must be very much dependent upon her companion, Mrs. Dane-Watford is particularly anxious to engage a lady who will be really kind and make her mother happy. Mrs. Dane-Watford will esteem it a great kindness if Mrs. Fellingborough will write quite frankly about Miss Jones.

THE JUMBLES,
DESSINGTON,
SHROPSHIRE.
(Date in full.)

Reply Respecting Miss Jones, Applicant for
Post as Lady-Companion.

Mrs. Fellingborough has much pleasure in replying to Mrs. Dane-Watford's enquiry about Miss Jones. During five years, when Mrs. Fellingborough was mostly an invalid, Miss Jones had much of the management of the house left in her hands, and she showed herself most capable and kindly in all that she did. She is a pleasant companion, well-read, and certainly a lady in every sense of the word. Mrs. Fellingborough feels sure that Mrs. Dane-Watford may feel perfectly at ease in engaging Miss Jones as companion to her mother.

FIR-TREE HOUSE,
NORTHFIELDS.
(Date in full.)

Application for Post as Nursery Governess.

Miss Emma Eastling writes in answer to advertisement in the *Church Times* for a nursery governess for two little boys. Miss Eastling is well accustomed to the care of young children, being herself the eldest of a family of eight, and is fond of children. She is well educated, attended the Dulwich High School from the time she was ten years old until she left school at the age of seventeen, and since then has lived at home and helped generally with the care of the house and her younger brothers and sisters. Miss Eastling is twenty-two years of age, is very healthy, and fond of outdoor life. Miss Eastling belongs to the English Church, and is allowed to name the Rev. Thomas B ——, the Vicar of this parish, as a reference, and can also confidently refer the advertiser to the Head Mistress of the High School she has attended. Will be glad to meet the advertiser for an interview if desired

3, FITZ-CLARENCE ROAD,
DULMINSTER.
(Date in full.)

Application for Post of Science Teacher in a Large School.

Miss Ethel Roberts has just heard from Messrs. Trueman and Henry that Miss Rickman is requiring a Science teacher in her school at Carnforth. Miss Roberts was a student at Newnham, and took Second Class Honours in the Natural Science Tripos in 19—, special subjects Chemistry, Physics, Biology, and Botany. Since then Miss Roberts has been resident in Cambridge for three years, giving daily lessons—in the mornings to the daughters of Professor Jinks of Clare, and in the afternoons to the daughters of the Rev. T. Binks, Classical Tutor of St. John's. Miss Roberts is desirous now of giving her time more entirely to scientific subjects, and is seeking just such an engagement as Miss Rickman appears to offer. Miss Roberts can give absolutely reliable references, and has excellent testimonials from Mrs. Jinks and the Rev. T. Binks, as well as from some of her former lecturers. Is thirty-one years of age and a member of the Church of England. Miss Roberts understands that Miss Rickman offers £125 a year, to be raised £10 after the first year. Should Miss Rickman entertain this application, Miss Roberts will be happy to meet her for a personal interview in town at any time Miss Rickman names.

12, MARYBOROUGH ROAD, N. 17
(Date in fall.)

Reply to Lady's Answer to an Advertisement re Post as Head-Nurse where there are Three Children.

SUFFOLK LODGE,
LESSINGBOROUGH.
(Date in full.)

DEAR MADAM,

I thank you for your reply to my advertisement for post as head-nurse. In my present engagement, which I am leaving on the 15th of next month, I have had entire charge of the nursery since the birth of the youngest little girl, who is now five years old, and for whom Lady C —— is engaging a French nursery governess. There are besides three older children—a boy who is now six and a half years, and twins, a boy and girl eight years old. I have had one under-nurse, and an under-housemaid has had the care, under my direction, of the nurseries. I am glad to be able to say that the children are all thoroughly healthy, and have ailed but very little since I took charge of them. Lady C —— is kind enough to say that she will be glad to recommend me: I can also give other quite satisfactory references. I am naturally very fond of children, and have had to do with them all my life. Before coming here I was second-nurse with the Honble. Mrs. Rhys, where there were four children in the nursery. I remained there for three years. I am thirty-two years of age, and have very good health. I shall be able to enter upon another engagement by the 31st of next month. May I ask you to be so very kind as to let me know as soon as possible if you would like to see me, as I have other answers to my advertisement? Salary required, £45 a year; and if any special uniform is to be worn, £5 a year for uniform.

I am,

Dear Madam,

Yours faithfully,

MARIAN RUSSELL.

Enquiry respecting Marian Russell, who is applying for Post as Head-Nurse.

Mrs. William Fossett-Browne would be exceedingly obliged if Lady C —— will kindly tell her what she knows of Miss Marian Russell as a head-nurse. Is she thoroughly healthy, truthful, and trustworthy? has her care of the nursery been satisfactory to Lady C —— ? and are the children happy in her care? Miss Russell states that she has had charge of Lady C ——'s nursery for five years, and that the children's health has been good during that time. May Mrs. Fossett-Browne rely upon that statement? and can Lady C —— thoroughly recommend Miss Russell as head-nurse?

BRUSSINGTON HALL,

NORTHBOROUGH.

(Date in full.)

Application for Post as Private Governess.

Miss Mary Jevons writes in answer to advertisement from Lady B —— in to-day's *Morning Post* for a governess for her two little girls, requiring French and Italian and usual English subjects.

Miss Jevons was educated at Cheltenham College; she then spent two years in Paris, giving English lessons, and before returning to England travelled for two months with one of her Parisian pupils in Italy, three weeks of that time living in Rome. At the present time, and during the last three years, Miss Jevons has been living as private governess in the family of the Honble. Mrs. Rainforth, teaching her two daughters, aged twelve and thirteen, and little boy of eight. Mrs. Rainforth is now making other family arrangements, and intends sending her children to school after the holidays, so that Miss Jevons will be disengaged after Easter; and Mrs. Rainforth is kind enough to say that she will be glad to recommend Miss Jevons for any similar engagement for which she wishes to apply— and Miss Jevons can also give other absolutely reliable references. Miss Jevons is twenty-nine years of age, and is a Churchwoman. Should the advertiser consider this application, Miss Jevons will be pleased to meet her for a personal interview at any hour and place that she will name. Miss Jevons would wish for a few weeks' holiday after leaving Haverstock Hall before taking up new work. Salary, £70 a year resident, or £120 non-resident, and the usual holidays to be arranged for.

Letter of Recommendation for Miss Mary Jevons as Private Governess.

The Honble. Mrs. Rainforth has much pleasure in recommending Miss Mary Jevons as private governess in a family. Miss Jevons lived with Mrs. Rainforth for three years as governess to her two daughters, who are now twelve and thirteen years old, and her little boy, aged eight; she gained the affection and respect and the entire confidence of the children, and proved herself an excellent teacher, as shown by all three children now taking very good places in the schools where they are—indeed, their French and general language and English composition, etc., have been specially remarked upon by their present teachers. It was with very great regret that Mrs. Rainforth parted from Miss Jevons when other arrangements had to be made for the children.

HAVERSTOCK HALL,
RUTLAND.
(*Date in full.*)

SECTION VI.

Letters of Congratulation and Condolence.

Congratulations on Safe Return of Husband from Being a Prisoner of War.

DEAR MRS. ROBINSON,

I am compelled to write at once to tell you how very glad I am to hear of Colonel Robinson's safe return. Mr. Watford, who, of course, joins with me most heartily in congratulations, brought the news home yesterday evening, and I could hardly refrain from running over there and then to see you both and shake hands with your dear husband; but I knew that, of course, you must have the first day or two quite to yourselves, and you will not want to be reading a long letter even from me or anyone. I suppose congratulations will be pouring in! I do hope the Colonel has not suffered beyond repair, and that in his own home and in your hands he will soon get strong again, and be in the way to forget the terrible past. Do give him my very warmest regards and remembrances and rejoicing with you with all my heart,

Believe me,
Ever your sincere friend,
ELEANOR WATFORD

Congratulations on the Engagement of Eldest Daughter.

SURBITON HALL,
NORTHMINSTER.
(Date in full.)

DEAR MRS. BLAKE-JEVONS,

May I, as an old friend, send you my congratulations on dear Cicely's engagement to the Honble. Captain Devensey, which I saw announced in *The Times* yesterday? It is, I am sure, a source of pleasure to you all, and Captain Devensey has been known to you for so long that you will be feeling so happy about the future for your dear girl. Do give my love and very best and kindest wishes to Cicely. I feel sure it is a heart to heart betrothal, and promises every happiness to them both. With very kindest regards from John and myself,

Believe me,
Ever yours affectionately,
SARAH ROSSITER.

Letter of Congratulation to a Girl on her Engagement.

HANNINGTON HOUSE,
WEST SHELFORD.
(Date in full.)

MY DEAR JENNIE,

I must send you a little line to tell you how glad I am to learn of your engagement to Willie Parminter. He is a great friend of my Cousin Arthur, and we all like him so much. Arthur told my husband yesterday (how these men do love a bit of gossip!), and I felt I must write at once because we are really so glad both for him and for you. Will you come and see me when you can and tell me all about it, and if any time is fixed yet? Of course, I want to know everything at once. Give my love to your dear mother. God bless you, my dear child, and with fondest love,

> Believe me,
> Ever your real friend,
> MABEL DARTFORD.

Congratulations on the Birth of First Grandchild.

TESSINGTON MANOR HOUSE,
SHROPSHIRE.
(Date in full.)

MY DEAR MRS. GILLINGHAM-LAKE,

Do accept my congratulations to you on the honour of becoming a grandmother, which I know you will fully appreciate—the honour, I mean, *not* my congratulations! I was so delighted to hear that dear Julia had started off with a son, and I hear that he is a very bonny boy! How proud you will be I very well know! I am dying for the time to come when I may go and see Julia and her son. Have they decided on a name yet? I am so glad to know that Julia has Mrs. Billing for a nurse. I believe she is excellent. Please give my love and congratulations to Julia when you see her, and please do let me know how she and the darling baby are going on.

Kindest regards from
Yours affectionately,
MILDRED SEVERS.

Condolence on the Death of Husband.

JERSINGHAM HALL,
WHICHMINSTER.
(Date in full.)

MY DEAR MRS. WESTON,

Were it not that I hope you look upon me as a very real friend I would hardly dare to intrude upon you now, even to assure you of my most heartfelt sympathy. May I say that I can hardly tell you how deeply I am feeling with you and for you, though I know truly "The heart alone knoweth its own bitterness," and there seems, perhaps, little or no ray of light on any side. Dear, I know that, too, so well. I will say no more, but only assure you again of my love and sympathy and prayers for you. Can I do anything at all for you in any way? You have only to let me know what it is.

All Whichminster feel they have lost a real friend.

With my very dear love,
Yours ever affectionately,
EFFIE STERNHOLD.

Condolence on the Death of a Sister.

BYWATER LODGE,
OUSEDALE,
YORKS.
(Date in full.)

MY DEAREST AGNES,

I cannot tell you how deeply grieved I am about your dear sister. I knew Molly was very ill, of course, and was hoping to get over and see you both, but I did not realize that the end could possibly come like this, and so soon. I know, dear, what a terrible loss it will be to you, and what it will mean; she was such a dear, dear girl. I always felt she was so good, and so thoughtful for others always. There will be very many who will miss her besides her own family You will let me know, won't you, if there is any thing at all that I can do for you. And with much love,

Believe me,
Yours always affectionately,
HELEN BAGSTER.

Condolence on the Loss of a Child.

LINGFORD,
NR. EASTMINSTER.
(Date in full.)

MY DEAR, DEAR KITTY,

I cannot help sending you a line, though I think you will hardly care to hear from anyone; but I do sorrow with you, dearest, and my heart is aching too! No one can fathom your sorrow, I know, except One, and so I can only kneel for you and ask that you may know the only real Comfort there is at such a time; and darling Jacky is safe now, and out of all temptation. God bless him and you!

With my fondest love,
Yours ever affectionately,
MILLICENT FOTHERINGHAM.

SECTION VII.

How to Begin and End a Letter.

King or Queen.

Address—To the King's (or Queen's) Most Excellent Majesty. *Begin*—Sire, *or* May it please your Majesty. *End*—I am, Sire (or Madam), your Majesty's most faithful and dutiful servant. Refer to as your Majesty always in body of letter.

Prince or Princess of Wales.

Address—To His Royal Highness the Prince of Wales (or to Her Royal Highness the Princess of Wales). *Begin*—Sir (or Madam), *or* May it please your Royal Highness. *End*—I am, Sir (or Madam), your Royal Highness's most obedient servant. Refer to as your Royal Highness.

Duke or Duchess.

Address—To His Grace the Duke of —— (or Her Grace the Duchess of ——). *Begin*—My Lord Duke (or Madam). *End*—I am, My Lord Duke (or Madam), your Grace's most devoted servant. Refer to as your Grace.

Duke's Children.

A Duke's daughter is addressed as The Right Honble. Lady (Maud) ——. Madam, ending as above.

The eldest son of a Duke ranks by courtesy as Peer, and takes the second title of his father. Refer to as your Lordship.

A Duke's widow ranks as Duchess, and becomes Duchess Dowager when the next Peer marries. She is addressed as Her Grace the Dowager Duchess of ——.

A Duke's younger son is addressed as The Right Honble. Lord (John) ——.

Marquis or Marchioness.

Address—To the Most Noble the Marquis (or the Marchioness) of ——. *Begin*—My Lord Marquis (or Madam). *End*—I am, My Lord Marquis, your Lordship's (or Madam, your Ladyship's) most obedient servant. Refer to as your Lordship or your Ladyship.

Earl or Countess.

Address—To the Right Honourable the Earl (or Countess) of ——. *Begin*—My Lord (or Madam). *End*—I am, My Lord, your Lordship's (or Madam, your Ladyship's) most obedient servant.

Viscount or Viscountess.

Address—To the Right Honourable the Viscount (or the Viscountess) ——. *Begin*—My Lord (or Madam). *End* as for Earl.

Baron or Baroness.

Address—To the Right Honourable the Lord (or the Baroness) ——. *Begin* and *End* as for Earl.

Baronets and Knights and their Wives.

Address—To Sir Arthur Browne, Bart.; To Lady Browne; To Sir Sidney H. Waterlow; To Lady Waterlow. *Begin*—Sir (or Madam). *End*—I am, Sir (or Madam), your obedient servant.

Officers of State, Governors, Ambassadors, Secretaries, Consuls, etc.

Address—To the Right Honourable Albert Gordon, His Majesty's Principal Secretary of State for the War Department. *Address*—To his Excellency the Right Honourable the Earl —— Lord Lieutenant of Ireland. *Begin*—My Lord, or according to rank. *End*—I have the honour to be, my Lord, your Lordship's most obedient servant.

Address—To His Excellency the Right Honourable (or according to rank), His Britannic Majesty's Envoy Extraordinary and Ambassador Plenipotentiary to the ——.

Address—To Henry Hawkins, Esq., Secretary to the United States Legation. *Address*—George Anderson, Esq., Consul to His Britannic Majesty at Tien-tsin. *Begin*—Sir. *End*—I have the honour to be, Sir, your obedient servant.

Treasury and Admiralty Officials.

Address—To the Lords Commissioners of His Majesty's Treasury; To the Lords Commissioners of the Admiralty. *Begin*—My Lords. *End*—I have the honour to be, my Lords, your Lordships' obedient servant.

Customs or Excise.

Address—To the Commissioners of His Majesty's Customs, or to the Commissioners of His Majesty's Inland Revenue. *Begin*—Gentlemen. *End*—I have the honour to be, Gentlemen, your obedient servant.

War Department.

Address—(usually) To the Under-Secretary of State for War. *Begin*—Sir, I have the honour, etc. *End*—In similar form.

Prime Minister and Privy Councillors.

The Prime Minister is addressed according to rank, but in any case as The Right Honourable the Prime Minister.

Privy Councillors as Right Honourable, and according to rank.

Cardinal.

Address—To His Eminence, William Edward Cardinal Archbishop of ——. *Begin*—Your Eminence.

A Cardinal ranks as a Prince of the Roman Catholic Church.

Archbishops of England and Ireland.

Address—To his Grace the Lord Archbishop of Canterbury. To the Right Reverend the Lord Bishop of London. *Begin*—My Lord Archbishop, My Lord Bishop. *End*—I remain, with the greatest respect, My Lord Archbishop, your Grace's devoted servant. I have the honour to be, my Lord Bishop, your Lordship's humble servant.

The full ceremonious title and address of the Archbishop of Canterbury is "The Most Reverend Father in God (David) by Divine Providence Lord Archbishop of Canterbury".

The Archbishop of York is addressed "by Divine Permission".

The Primate of Ireland would be addressed as "His Grace the Lord Primate of Ireland".

Lord Mayor.

Address—The Right Honourable the Lord Mayor of ——, *or* The Right Honourable Sir Elphinstow Jackson, Lord Mayor of ——. *Begin* and *End* as to a Baron.

Companions of Orders of Knighthood are addressed as So-and-so, Esq., C.B., or C.M.G., as may be.

If Knights, with K.C.B. or other distinction affixed, as—Sir James Elphinstone, K.C.B., C.S.I.

Bishop.

Bishops are Right Reverend —— the Lord Bishop of ——, *or* The Right Reverend the Bishop Suffragan; *or* The Lord Bishop of ——. *Letters begin*—Right Reverend Sir, *or* My Lord. *Letters end*—I have the honour to be, Right Reverend Sir, or My Lord, your obedient servant.

Colonial Bishops as English Bishops.

Wives of Bishops are addressed as ordinary ladies in Society. The rank of their husband gives no courtesy address.

Deans and Archdeacons.

Address—To the Very Reverend the Dean of York, *or* To the Venerable the Archdeacon. *Begin*—Very Reverend Sir, *or* Venerable Sir. *End*—I have the honour to be, Very Reverend Sir, *or* Venerable Sir, your obedient servant.

Clergymen and Ministers.

Address—If the son of a Duke, as The Reverend Lord (John) ——, adding degrees or titles. If son of an Earl, The Reverend The Honourable Alan ——. A Clergyman or Minister who is a Commoner is addressed as The Reverend Stephen ——. *Begin*—Reverend Sir. *End*—I have the honour to be, Sir (as usual).

Naval and Military Officers.

Address—(with titles according to rank) Admiral the Honourable ——, C.B., *or* General the Right Honourable ——, G.C.B. Captain *or* Commander ——, R.N. Major Gerrard, V.C.

Lieutenants in the Navy or Army are addressed as Arthur Appline, Esq., R.N., *or* Gerald Hayes, Esq., R.E.

When members of the *Medical Profession* have the M.D. degree, affix it, and address them as Esquires—John Wallace Kemp, Esq., M.D. Surgeons are addressed as Mr., *not* Doctor.

Lord Chancellor.

Address—To the Right Honourable the Lord High Chancellor of Great Britain. *Begin* and *End* as to a Peer of similar rank.

Lord Chief Justice.

Address—To the Right Honourable the Lord Chief Justice of England.